AWESOME ANIMALS

By Gina Ingoglia

Illustrated by Turi MacCombie

A GOLDEN BOOK • NEW YORK

Western Publishing Company, Inc., Racine, Wisconsin 53404

Wherever you go, you will find animals. You can go up to the highest mountain. You can go down into the lowest valley. You can go to places where it is very, very hot and almost nothing grows or to places where it is so cold, it snows all the time. You will find animals living in all of these places. And some of these animals are truly *awesome*!

AWESOME ANIMALS

Note: On page 48 there is a list of some of the words in this book and how to say them.

A dragon is a make-believe animal that breathes out fire and smoke.

A **Komodo dragon** is a real animal. It looks a little like a make-believe dragon. It's the biggest lizard in the world. Full-grown males weigh as much as three hundred pounds and some are as long as a rowboat. So even if they don't breathe fire, Komodo dragons can still be pretty scary.

Komodo dragons are fierce fighters. They have strong legs and a powerful tail. These huge lizards kill and eat animals as large as deer and wild boar.

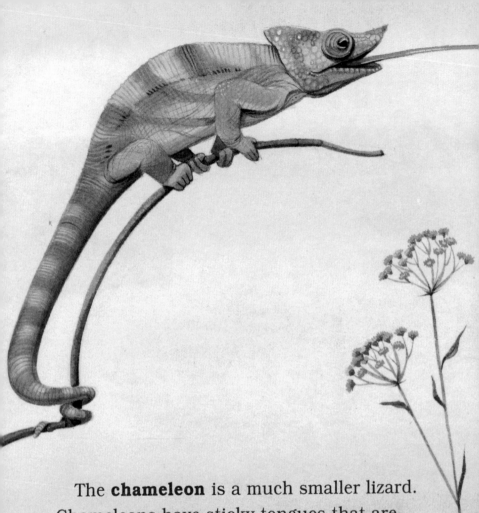

The **chameleon** is a much smaller lizard.
Chameleons have sticky tongues that are
longer than their bodies. When they are not
eating, chameleons keep their tongues rolled
up inside their mouths. When they get
hungry, they shoot out their long tongues to
catch insects.

Light, heat, and cold make chameleons' bumpy skin change color! Sometimes chameleons change color to frighten their enemies. They also scare their enemies by puffing up their bodies and hissing like snakes.

Chameleons can look in two directions at the same time! They do this by moving each eye by itself.

Tarsiers' bodies are only about as long as your hand. But their tails are twice as long. Their unusual feet help them get from tree to tree. They have flat, round toes with strong suction pads at their tips. Tarsiers leap from one tree to another. They land on a tree trunk and hold on with their toes. Sometimes they even sleep holding tight to a tree!

Little tarsiers also have strange eyes. Their eyes are huge so that the animals can see in the dark. To watch for danger, tarsiers can turn their heads almost completely around in a circle.

Vampire bats sleep hanging upside down! They hang from cave walls using the sharp claws on their toes.

Yes, it's true. Vampire bats really do drink blood. At night they fly out of their caves and suck blood from sleeping animals. Vampire bats land so softly, the animals are probably unaware that they have been bitten when they wake up.

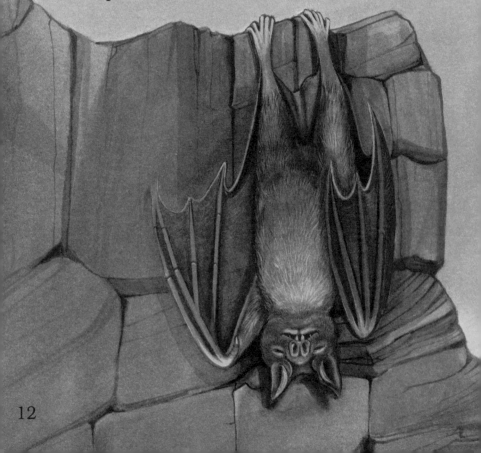

A vampire bat can fly, but it has unusual
wings. Loose, thin skin is spread between
the bat's long fingers. The skin is also
stretched between its hind legs and tail.
When the fingers and legs are spread, the
skin is pulled tight. With these wings, the
bat is ready to fly.

This animal doesn't really fly. It glides!
The **giant flying squirrel**'s legs and tail are
joined together by loose skin. The squirrel
opens its four legs as it leaps into the air.
The loose skin spreads out and catches the
air under it.

This squirrel lives in the jungle trees.
Not many people have seen one because
the squirrels hunt at night.

The **flying snake** can also glide. Before it takes off, a flying snake breathes out all the air in its body. It spreads itself out and becomes very flat. Then it springs into the air and heads for another tree!

This is one of the laziest animals in the world. The **three-toed sloth** doesn't fly. It hardly even moves! It sleeps hanging from a tree!

A baby sloth lies on its mother's chest. It sleeps most of the time, too.

A sloth's fur looks green. That's because tiny plants grow in it!

Koalas also spend lots of time in trees. A baby koala will often ride on its mother's back as she moves from tree to tree.

Koalas will only eat leaves from eucalyptus trees. These leaves have a strong odor. Because they eat so many of them, koalas smell like the leaves! Imagine eating so many pickles that you smelled like a pickle!

The **giant panda** looks like a big black-and-white bear. But it is not a bear. It belongs to the raccoon family. Pandas live in the high mountains and have thick fur to keep them warm.

Giant pandas eat sitting up. Most of the
time they eat only bamboo. Pandas hold on
to the bamboo with a pad on their paws. The
pad works like your thumb. This is very rare
in the animal world.

When giant panda babies are born, they
are no bigger than mice. Someday they may
weigh three hundred pounds!

These babies have white stripes when they
are born. The stripes go away as the **wild
boar** gets older.

A wild boar can smell its favorite food—
roots—growing under the ground. It digs
them up with its tough nose.

A long, sharp tooth grows from each side of a boar's mouth. These teeth are called tusks. Tusks help in digging. They are also used for fighting. Wild boars are strong fighters.

The male **proboscis monkey** is really
strange to look at. He has regular teeth,
but he also has a *huge* nose! The nose is
so big that when the monkey eats, his nose
often gets in the way.

But this nose comes in handy when danger
is near. Then the monkey makes a honking
sound with his nose. This warns other
monkeys. When it honks, the proboscis
monkey's nose gets stiff and sticks out.

Proboscis monkeys spend lots of time sitting in the sun. Then they like to cool off in the water. They can swim and dive just like people can.

Kudus also live in hot places. They live
together with lots of other kudus. A group
of kudus is called a herd.

Kudus have very long, curved horns that they use in fighting. But kudus often have to run from danger. These graceful animals leap high in the air while they run. This makes kudus a lot harder for lions or other hungry animals to catch!

The powerful **musk ox** lives in cold, snowy lands. Its long, shaggy fur keeps out the cold air and wind. The musk ox also has horns. With these heavy, sharp horns, the musk ox can fight fiercely.

Musk oxen are very smart. Sometimes a hungry wolf tries to attack a herd of musk oxen. Then the whole herd forms a circle around the calves to keep them safe inside. Each musk ox faces outside. This makes a circle of sharp horns, all pointing at the wolf. No wolf wants to fight that!

The **black rhinoceros** has tough skin and *two* sharp horns to protect itself. It is one of the strongest and fiercest of all animals.

Rhinos don't see very well. But they never run from danger. They stand and fight. Even a hungry lion will leave a big rhino alone!

Rhinos live in lands where the sun gets
very hot. They like to roll in the mud. The
mud cools off their skin and keeps bugs away.

The **mongoose** is also a fighting animal. It sometimes fights a huge snake called a **cobra**. The fight may last for hours.

The cobra rises up and spreads out its neck. It strikes out at the mongoose with its fangs full of poison. If the snake bites the mongoose, the mongoose will die.

The quick mongoose dances around—just
far enough away so the cobra can't reach it.
When the snake gets tired, the mongoose
makes its move. The mongoose tries to bite
the cobra near its head to kill it.

When a cobra and mongoose fight, the
clever mongoose almost always wins!

When faced with danger, the **basilisk lizard** stands up on its back legs and runs away. This speedy lizard can even run across water! There are three reasons why the lizard doesn't sink. Its body is very light. It has big feet and fringes on its toes to hold it up. And it moves very fast.

These animals live near rivers and lakes and in hot, wet lands called swamps. **Crocodiles** spend lots of time in the water but also like to lie in the sun.

A crocodile's eyes, ears, and nose are on top of its head. While the rest of its body is underwater, the creature can still see, hear, and breathe. This lets it sneak up on other animals. The crocodile can swim close to the shore without being seen. Then, with a snap of its huge jaws, the hungry crocodile grabs a large bird and takes it underwater to eat.

35

The **Arabian camel**, or dromedary, never goes in the water. It lives in a hot, sandy land called a desert.

Camels are made for desert life! They don't need food or water for days. They drink gallons of water at one time and store fat for energy in the large hump on their backs.

Sand is a real problem in the desert. Camels shut their noses tight to keep out the blowing sand. A special third eyelid helps keep the sand out of their eyes. To keep them from sinking into the soft sand, camels have broad, thick feet.

37

This animal needs to eat a lot every day. Usually a **giant anteater** eats about thirty thousand insects a day! Anteaters have tiny mouths and no teeth. They have a sticky tongue that looks like a very long worm! Anteaters use their tongue to pick up ants and termites.

Termites and ants live inside mounds made of hard dirt. When an anteater gets hungry, it breaks a mound open with its sharp claws. Then the animal puts its tongue into the mound and pulls out hundreds of ants at a time—all stuck to its long tongue!

Giant anteaters have no home. They sleep in the grass all day and hunt at night.

The **giraffe** is the tallest animal on earth. It can run faster than a horse. It lives in grassy lands and can go without water for several weeks.

Giraffes eat plants. With their long necks, they can reach leaves growing high on trees. Their long tongues and strong lips are not bothered by prickly thorns.

These tall giraffes can see far away and often warn other animals of danger.

These animals are very low to the ground. **Giant land tortoises** look like big turtles and may weigh up to five hundred pounds. Turtles spend some time in water. Tortoises live only on land.

One kind of giant land tortoise eats plants growing close to the ground. Its shell is shaped like the shells of other turtles and tortoises.

Another kind of giant land tortoise eats leaves growing on small trees. Its shell is shaped so the tortoise can stretch its long neck. It can reach plants growing above its head.

When danger is near, the huge tortoises pull their heads and legs inside the hard shells for protection.

The **nine-banded armadillo** is covered
with nine plates that are hard as bones. The
plates fit together so the animal can bend its
body. To protect itself, an armadillo can roll
into a hard ball. Then even its head and tail
are safely tucked inside! It stays rolled up
until the danger is gone.

Armadillos have strong claws. They dig holes to live in or to get away from danger. They also use their claws to dig up insects and worms.

Nine-banded armadillo females always have four babies at a time. The babies are either all males or all females.

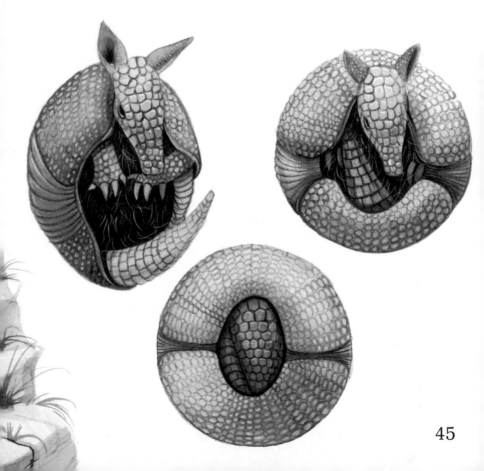

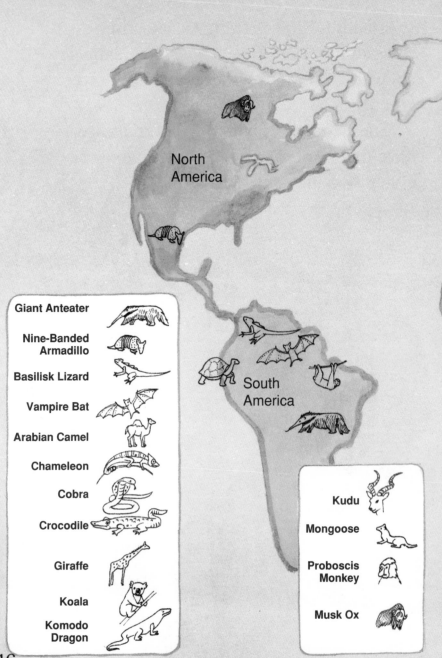

North America

South America

Giant Anteater

Nine-Banded Armadillo

Basilisk Lizard

Vampire Bat

Arabian Camel

Chameleon

Cobra

Crocodile

Giraffe

Koala

Komodo Dragon

Kudu

Mongoose

Proboscis Monkey

Musk Ox

The animals in this book come from all over the world. This map shows you some of the places where they live.

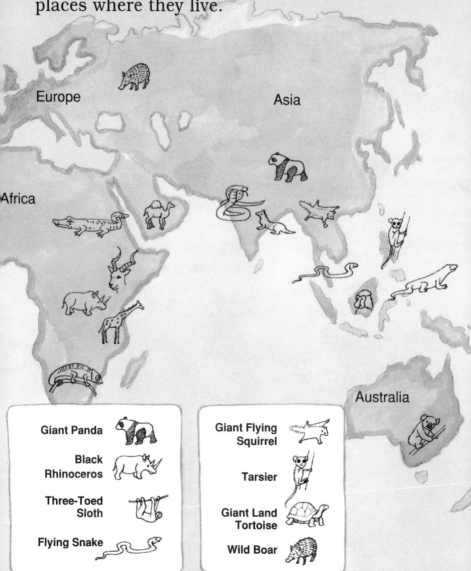

Europe

Asia

Africa

Australia

Giant Panda

Black Rhinoceros

Three-Toed Sloth

Flying Snake

Giant Flying Squirrel

Tarsier

Giant Land Tortoise

Wild Boar

Here are some of the words from this book and how to say them.

Arabian Camel	(ah RAY be in CAM ull)
Armadillo	(arm uh DIL lo)
Basilisk Lizard	(BASS ih lisk LIZ urd)
Boar	(bore)
Chameleon	(cah MEEL yun)
Creature	(CREE chur)
Crocodile	(CROCK uh dile)
Dromedary	(DROM uh dare ee)
Eucalyptus	(u ka LIP tuss)
Giraffe	(jeh RAFF)
Koala	(ko AL la)
Komodo Dragon	(ko MO doe DRAG un)
Kudu	(KOO doo)
Poison	(POY zin)
Proboscis	(pro BOS siss)
Rhinoceros	(ry NOSS seh russ)
Sloth	(slawth)
Tarsier	(TAR see year)
Tortoise	(TOR tiss)
Vampire Bat	(VAM pie er BAT)